A Comprehensive Guide to Women's Safety

C. P. Kumar
Reiki Healer
Roorkee - 247667, India

Disclaimer

While every effort has been made to ensure the accuracy and completeness of the content in this book, the author cannot guarantee that the information contained herein is error-free, up-to-date, or suitable for every individual circumstance.

The author shall not be held liable or responsible for any errors or omissions in the content of the book, nor for any damages, or losses that may arise from any actions taken based upon the suggestions or contents presented in the book.

Readers are advised to use their own judgment and discretion in applying the information provided in this book, and to consult with qualified professionals before taking any action based on the contents of this book. The author disclaims any and all liability or responsibility for any actions taken or not taken based on the information contained in this book.

DEDICATION

To the women who have endured, persevered, and triumphed, and to those who aspire to a world where their safety is not compromised.

In dedication to the indomitable spirit of women everywhere, this book, "A Comprehensive Guide to Women's Safety", is lovingly dedicated. Your strength, resilience, and determination in the face of adversity inspire us to create a safer world for all. May your courage serve as a beacon, guiding us towards a future where women can live free from fear, violence, and discrimination.

In the pages that follow, we endeavor to equip you with knowledge, tools, and strategies to enhance your safety, empower you to stand up against injustice, and help you become architects of change in your communities. This book is a tribute to your unwavering commitment to a world where every woman can flourish and fulfill her potential.

We dedicate this book to:

- ❖ The survivors, whose stories remind us of the strength of the human spirit.
- ❖ The advocates, who tirelessly work to transform policies and systems for the better.
- ❖ The mentors, who inspire the next generation to dream bigger and reach higher.
- ❖ The global community, united in the pursuit of gender equality and women's rights.

May the words within these chapters serve as a testament to our shared commitment to women's safety and the collective responsibility we bear in ensuring a brighter, safer future for all.

With boundless admiration and dedication,

C. P. Kumar

CONTENTS

PREFACE

In a world where every individual should feel safe and secure, the reality is that not everyone enjoys the same level of safety. Women, in particular, face unique challenges and vulnerabilities that demand our attention and action. It is within this context that we present "A Comprehensive Guide to Women's Safety".

The importance of this topic cannot be overstated. Ensuring the safety and security of women is not just a moral imperative but a fundamental human right. Yet, it is a sad truth that women continue to face various threats – physical, emotional, and online – that infringe upon their well-being and hinder their ability to lead fulfilling lives. This book is an ambitious endeavor to shed light on the multifaceted dimensions of women's safety, equipping women with knowledge, tools, and resources to protect themselves and thrive.

Within these pages, you will embark on a journey through the myriad aspects of women's safety and security. From understanding the various threats women face, delving into the legal framework that safeguards their rights, and exploring practical personal safety measures, to addressing critical issues such as domestic violence, online harassment, and workplace discrimination, this comprehensive guide leaves no stone unturned.

We also recognize the importance of community support networks, mental and emotional well-being, education, empowerment, and advocacy in fostering a safer environment for women. As such, we have included chapters that provide guidance on building a support network, coping with trauma, accessing education and skill development, and engaging with policymakers to drive change.

Our exploration extends beyond borders, acknowledging that women's safety is a global concern. We delve into the worldwide issues that affect women, the international efforts and organizations working to address them, and the importance of cross-cultural considerations in finding effective solutions.

This book aims not only to inform but to inspire. Each chapter aims to empower women to take control of their safety by providing practical advice and valuable resources. We believe that knowledge is the first step towards change, and it is our hope that this guide will motivate individuals to take action, advocate for women's rights, and contribute to creating a safer world for all.

In conclusion, "A Comprehensive Guide to Women's Safety" is not just a book; it is a call to action. It is an invitation to join us in the pursuit of a world where every woman can live her life free from fear and insecurity. Together, let us embark on this journey, armed with knowledge, compassion, and determination, as we work towards a safer, more equitable future for women everywhere.

C. P. Kumar
Reiki Healer
Former Scientist 'G', National Institute of Hydrology
Roorkee - 247667, India
Web: https://www.angelfire.com/nh/cpkumar/virgo.html

Chapter 1. Introduction to Women's Safety and Security

Women's safety and security are paramount concerns in today's world. While significant progress has been made in recent decades to empower and protect women, there is still much work to be done to ensure that every woman can live free from fear and violence. This comprehensive guide, titled "A Comprehensive Guide to Women's Safety", aims to shed light on various aspects of women's safety and security, equipping women with knowledge and resources to navigate a world that is not always safe or fair. In this introductory chapter, we will explore the importance of the topic, the scope of the book, and provide a historical perspective on women's safety.

The Importance of the Topic

Women's safety is not just a women's issue; it is a societal issue that affects us all. Ensuring the safety and security of women is essential for building a just and equitable society. When women feel safe, they are more likely to participate fully in education, the workforce, and public life. This, in turn, contributes to the overall development and progress of a nation.

However, the sad reality is that women around the world face a multitude of threats on a daily basis. These threats come in various forms, including physical violence, emotional abuse, online harassment, and discrimination. Violence against women is a global epidemic that knows no boundaries of age, race, or socio-economic status. It hinders women's potential and perpetuates cycles of fear and trauma.

Gender-Based Violence: One of the most pressing issues related to women's safety is gender-based violence. Women around the world face various forms of violence, including domestic violence, sexual harassment, assault, and human trafficking. Addressing these issues is crucial to protect women's physical and mental well-being.

Economic Empowerment: Women's safety is closely tied to their economic security. Gender discrimination in the workplace, unequal pay, and limited access to economic resources can leave women financially vulnerable. Empowering women economically is essential for their long-term safety and independence.

Health and Reproductive Rights: Women's safety also extends to their health and reproductive rights. Access to healthcare, family planning, and safe childbirth are essential components of women's well-being. Lack of access to these services can jeopardize their safety and health.

Psychological and Emotional Well-being: Emotional and psychological safety is equally important. Discrimination, harassment, and societal expectations can have detrimental effects on women's mental health. Addressing these issues is essential for promoting overall safety and happiness.

The Scope of the Book

"A Comprehensive Guide to Women's Safety" is a comprehensive resource that addresses the multifaceted aspects of women's safety and security. This book is organized into 15 chapters, each dedicated to a specific dimension of women's safety. We will delve into topics such as understanding the threats women face, the legal framework protecting women's rights, personal safety, home and neighborhood safety, online safety, dating and relationships, workplace safety, community and support networks, mental and emotional well-being, education and empowerment, government and policy advocacy, the global perspective, and preventing violence against women. These chapters aim to provide women with practical knowledge, tools, and strategies to enhance their safety and security in various aspects of their lives.

Historical Perspective on Women's Safety

Understanding the historical context is crucial to appreciate the progress made in women's safety and the challenges that persist. Throughout history, women have faced various forms of oppression and discrimination that have shaped their experiences of safety and security.

Ancient Societies: In many ancient societies, women had limited rights and were often subjected to violence and discrimination. Their safety was contingent on their social status and the patriarchal norms of the time.

Suffrage Movement: The suffrage movement was a social and political campaign aimed at securing voting rights, particularly for women, and promoting equality in the democratic process. The struggle for women's suffrage in the late 19th and early 20th centuries was a pivotal moment in women's history. It marked the beginning of significant changes in women's rights and safety.

World Wars and Social Change: The world wars led to significant social changes, including increased employment opportunities for women. However, it also highlighted the challenges they faced in the workplace and at home.

Civil Rights Movement: The Civil Rights Movement was a social and political movement in the United States that aimed to end racial segregation and discrimination against African Americans, primarily during the 1950s and 1960s, through nonviolent protest and legal activism. The civil rights movement contributed to the broader discussion of equality and civil liberties. It influenced the women's liberation movement and laid the foundation for addressing issues of safety and discrimination.

Modern Challenges: Despite progress, modern society still grapples with issues of violence against women, workplace discrimination, and gender-based disparities. Understanding this history helps contextualize the ongoing struggle for women's safety.

Conclusion

Women's safety and security are fundamental human rights. This book, "A Comprehensive Guide to Women's Safety", aims to empower women with the knowledge and resources needed to protect themselves and advocate for their rights. By addressing various aspects of women's safety, from personal security to legal protections, we hope to contribute to a world where all women can live free from fear and violence.

In the chapters that follow, we will delve deeper into specific areas of women's safety, providing insights, advice, and actionable steps to enhance women's security in their daily lives. It is our belief that through education, empowerment, and collective action, we can work towards a future where women's safety is not a privilege but a universal reality. Together, we can create a world where every woman can thrive, unburdened by the shadows of fear and insecurity.

Introduction

Women's safety is an issue of paramount importance in today's world. While progress has been made towards gender equality, women continue to face a myriad of threats that compromise their well-being, security, and peace of mind. To address these threats effectively, it is crucial to gain a comprehensive understanding of the various forms of danger that women encounter daily. This article explores the multifaceted threats women face, including physical, emotional, and online threats, supported by statistics and data on violence against women.

Types of Threats Women Face

Physical Threats

Physical threats are perhaps the most visible and direct form of danger women confront. These threats encompass a wide range of behaviors, from street harassment to domestic violence and sexual assault. It is essential to recognize that physical threats can take on different forms and degrees of severity.

Street Harassment: Catcalling, stalking, and public harassment are everyday occurrences that women endure while navigating public spaces. Catcalling refers to the act of making unwanted, often sexually suggestive, comments or gestures towards someone in a public place, typically directed at women. Stalking is a pattern of unwanted, obsessive, and often intimidating or threatening behavior directed towards an individual, which may include following them, making unwanted contact, or monitoring their activities, causing the victim to feel fear, distress, or harassment. Stalking is a criminal offense in many jurisdictions. These actions contribute to a pervasive sense of insecurity and discomfort.

Domestic Violence: Many women suffer in silence within the confines of their homes, facing physical abuse from their intimate partners. This form of violence can be both physically and emotionally devastating, trapping victims in a cycle of fear and abuse.

Sexual Assault: Rape and sexual assault are traumatic experiences that leave lasting scars on victims. These crimes can occur in various settings, including homes, workplaces, or social gatherings.

Human Trafficking: Women and girls are particularly vulnerable to human trafficking, which involves abduction, coercion, and forced exploitation for labor or sexual purposes.

Honor Killings: In some cultures, women may face the threat of honor killings for perceived violations of societal norms. This practice is a tragic manifestation of gender-based violence.

Emotional Threats

Emotional threats are often less visible but equally damaging to a woman's mental and emotional well-being. These threats can take various forms, including:

Emotional Abuse: Manipulation, gaslighting, and constant criticism can erode a woman's self-esteem and sense of self-worth. Gaslighting is a form of psychological manipulation in which a person seeks to make another person doubt their own perceptions, memories, or sanity by denying or distorting facts, events, or reality, often to gain control or undermine the other person's confidence and self-esteem. Emotional abuse can occur within relationships, families, or workplaces.

Cyberbullying: In the digital age, women are susceptible to online harassment and cyberbullying. Cyberbullying is the use of digital communication tools, such as social media, texting, or email, to harass, threaten, or intimidate others, often with the intent to harm their reputation or emotional well-being. It can include spreading rumors, posting hurtful comments, sharing private information, or engaging in other forms of online harassment. Social media platforms can become breeding grounds for hate speech, threats, and cyberattacks.

Discrimination: Systemic discrimination and gender bias can negatively impact a woman's career, opportunities, and overall quality of life. This form of emotional threat is pervasive and often subtle.

Online Threats

The internet has brought both opportunities and challenges for women's safety. Online threats include:

Cyberstalking: Cyberstalking is a form of online harassment and stalking in which an individual uses the internet, social media, or electronic communication to repeatedly harass, threaten, or intimidate another person. It often involves intrusive and unwelcome behavior that can cause significant distress and fear to the victim. Cyberstalking can include actions such as sending threatening messages, tracking someone's online activities, or using technology to invade a person's privacy. Persistent online harassment and stalking can be deeply distressing, as perpetrators invade a woman's digital space and privacy.

Non-consensual Sharing of Intimate Content: The distribution of private, intimate images without consent, commonly known as "revenge porn", is a digital threat that can lead to emotional distress and reputational harm.

Online Hate Speech: Women are often targeted with hate speech and misogyny in online forums and social media platforms, perpetuating a toxic online environment.

Statistics and Data on Violence Against Women

To comprehend the gravity of the threats women face, it is imperative to consider the sobering statistics and data surrounding violence against women.

1. Domestic Violence

According to the World Health Organization (WHO), approximately 1 in 3 women worldwide has experienced physical or sexual intimate partner violence or non-partner sexual violence in their lifetime.

In the United States, nearly 20 people per minute are physically abused by an intimate partner, equating to more than 10 million women and men annually, as reported by the National Coalition Against Domestic Violence.

2. Sexual Assault

RAINN (Rape, Abuse & Incest National Network) is an American nonprofit organization that provides support, education, and resources for survivors of sexual assault and advocates for policies and initiatives to prevent sexual violence. RAINN reports that 1 in 6 women in the United States has experienced an attempted or completed rape in their lifetime.

Globally, the United Nations estimates that 35% of women have experienced either physical and/or sexual intimate partner violence or non-partner sexual violence.

3. Cyberbullying and Online Threats

A 2021 study by the Pew Research Center found that 41% of women aged 18 to 29 in the United States reported being personally subjected to online harassment.

Women, especially those from marginalized communities, are more likely to experience severe forms of online abuse, including doxxing and threats of physical violence. Doxxing, short for "dropping documents", is the malicious act of revealing and publishing a person's private or personal information, such as their name, address, phone number, or other sensitive data, often with the intention of harassing, threatening, or causing harm to the individual.

4. Workplace Discrimination

The gender pay gap persists in many parts of the world, with women earning, on average, 20% less than men, according to data from the World Economic Forum.

A 2019 study by https://leanin.org/ and McKinsey & Company revealed that women remain underrepresented in leadership positions, comprising only 21% of C-suite executives in the United States. C-suite executives are top-level executives in a company, typically holding titles that start with "Chief" (e.g., CEO - Chief Executive Officer, CFO - Chief Financial Officer) and are responsible for making high-level decisions and managing the overall direction and strategy of the organization.

Conclusion

Understanding the threats women face is an essential step toward creating a safer world for all. From physical violence to emotional abuse and online harassment, women confront a range of dangers that impact their physical and mental well-being. The statistics and data on violence against women are a stark reminder of the urgency to address these issues comprehensively.

To build a society where women can live free from fear and discrimination, it is crucial to enact legal reforms, promote gender equality, and foster a culture of respect and empathy. Everyone has a role to play in ensuring women's safety, whether by supporting survivors, advocating for change, or challenging harmful attitudes and behaviors. By recognizing the threats women face and working together to combat them, we can strive towards a world where women can live their lives without the burden of constant danger and insecurity.

Introduction

Women's safety is a fundamental human right that forms the bedrock of any civilized society. Ensuring the safety and well-being of women requires a robust legal framework that not only recognizes their rights but also provides a means of recourse in case those rights are violated. This article explores the legal framework for women's safety, encompassing laws and regulations that protect women's rights and the avenues available to victims seeking legal redress.

Laws and Regulations Protecting Women's Rights

1. Gender Equality Laws

Gender equality laws play a pivotal role in safeguarding women's rights. These laws are designed to eliminate discrimination on the basis of gender and promote equal opportunities for men and women in various spheres of life, including education, employment, and public services. In many countries, these laws serve as the foundation for ensuring women's safety by addressing the root causes of gender-based discrimination.

2. Domestic Violence Laws

Domestic violence is a pervasive issue that affects women of all ages, backgrounds, and social statuses. Laws against domestic violence are essential to protect women from physical, emotional, and economic abuse within their homes. These laws typically include provisions for restraining orders, emergency protection orders, and penalties for perpetrators of domestic violence.

3. Sexual Harassment Laws

Sexual harassment laws are designed to prevent and address unwelcome sexual advances, requests for sexual favors, and other forms of inappropriate behavior in the workplace and public spaces. These laws empower women to assert their rights and seek legal remedies when subjected to harassment, creating safer environments for all.

4. Human Trafficking Laws

Human trafficking is a heinous crime that disproportionately affects women and girls. Laws against human trafficking are crucial for combating the trafficking of women for sexual exploitation and forced labor. They provide the legal basis for prosecuting traffickers and protecting the rights of survivors.

5. Laws against Female Genital Mutilation (FGM)

Female Genital Mutilation (FGM) is the practice of altering or removing parts of the female genitalia for non-medical reasons. It is a harmful traditional practice that poses severe risks to the physical and psychological well-being of women and girls. Legal prohibitions against FGM are essential for eradicating this practice and protecting women from its harmful effects.

6. Reproductive Rights Laws

Reproductive rights laws ensure that women have control over their reproductive health and decisions. These laws encompass access to contraception, abortion services, and comprehensive sex education. They empower women to make informed choices about their bodies and reproductive futures.

7. Maternity and Paternity Leave Laws

Maternity and paternity leave laws contribute to women's safety by promoting work-life balance and supporting women in their roles as caregivers. These laws grant parents the right to take time off work to care for their newborns or adopted children, reducing the economic burden on women and allowing them to maintain their careers.

Legal Recourse for Victims

1. Reporting Incidents

One of the first steps in seeking legal recourse for victims of gender-based violence or discrimination is to report the incident to the appropriate authorities. This may involve contacting the police, human rights organizations, or workplace supervisors, depending on the nature of the violation.

2. Legal Aid and Support Services

Access to legal aid and support services is essential for women who cannot afford legal representation. Many countries provide free or subsidized legal assistance to victims of gender-based violence, ensuring that financial barriers do not prevent them from seeking justice.

3. Civil Lawsuits

Victims of gender-based discrimination or violence have the option to file civil lawsuits against the perpetrators. These lawsuits seek monetary compensation for the harm suffered and can serve as a deterrent to future violations.

4. Criminal Prosecution

Criminal prosecution is a vital tool for holding perpetrators of gender-based violence accountable for their actions. Laws against domestic violence, sexual assault, and human trafficking often result in criminal charges against the offenders, leading to penalties such as imprisonment.

5. Protective Orders

Many legal systems allow victims of domestic violence or stalking to obtain protective orders or restraining orders against their perpetrators. These orders can restrict the offender's contact with the victim, providing a layer of physical safety.

6. Supportive Legal Measures

In addition to punitive measures, legal systems often incorporate supportive measures such as counseling, therapy, and rehabilitation programs for both victims and offenders. These measures aim to address the root causes of violence and promote healing and recovery.

7. International Legal Mechanisms

Women facing violence or discrimination may seek recourse through international legal mechanisms, such as filing complaints with United Nations human rights bodies or regional organizations. These mechanisms can put pressure on governments to address violations of women's rights and provide redress to victims.

Conclusion

A comprehensive legal framework is essential for ensuring the safety and well-being of women. Laws and regulations that protect women's rights, such as gender equality laws, domestic violence laws, and sexual harassment laws, serve as the foundation for creating a more equitable society. Legal recourse options, including reporting incidents, accessing legal aid, pursuing civil lawsuits, and seeking criminal prosecution, provide victims with the means to seek justice and hold perpetrators accountable.

It is crucial to recognize that women's safety is not solely a matter of legal enforcement but also a cultural and societal shift towards respecting and valuing women's rights. Education, awareness, and advocacy play a vital role in complementing legal measures and fostering a culture of respect and equality.

In our ongoing efforts to create a world where women can live free from violence and discrimination, a robust and responsive legal framework remains a critical component. Empowering women to assert their rights and providing avenues for legal recourse are essential steps towards achieving gender equality and ensuring the safety of women in all aspects of life.

Introduction

Personal safety is a fundamental concern for everyone, regardless of gender. However, women often face unique challenges and safety concerns in their daily lives. In today's world, being proactive and well-prepared for various situations is crucial for ensuring personal safety. This article explores the essential aspects of personal safety for women, offering valuable insights and practical tips to help them navigate the world with confidence.

Self-defense Techniques and Training

1. Empowerment through Self-Defense

Self-defense is a vital aspect of personal safety. It empowers women with the knowledge and skills needed to protect themselves in potentially dangerous situations. Self-defense techniques can range from basic moves, such as learning how to break free from a wrist grab, to more advanced martial arts training.

2. Self-Defense Classes

Enrolling in self-defense classes is a proactive step towards personal safety. These classes teach practical techniques, improve physical fitness, and boost self-confidence. Women should seek reputable instructors and programs tailored to their needs.

3. Stay Mentally Prepared

Self-defense is not just about physical strength; it's also about mental preparedness. Developing a keen awareness of your surroundings and the ability to stay calm under pressure can be just as important as physical skills.

4. Carry Personal Safety Tools

Consider carrying personal safety tools such as pepper spray, personal alarms, or even a small flashlight. These tools can provide an added layer of protection in case of emergencies.

Situational Awareness

1. Understanding Situational Awareness

Situational awareness involves being fully aware of your surroundings and the people around you. It's a key element of personal safety, as it allows you to identify potential threats and make informed decisions.

2. Avoiding Risky Areas

One of the simplest ways to enhance situational awareness is to avoid high-risk areas, especially during late hours. Familiarize yourself with your local neighborhood and identify safe routes to walk or drive.

3. Trusting Your Gut Instinct

Women often have a strong intuition. Trust your instincts; if something feels off or makes you uncomfortable, remove yourself from the situation immediately.

4. Staying Connected

Maintain open lines of communication with friends and family. Share your whereabouts and plans, so someone always knows your location. Consider using safety apps that allow friends or family to track your location in real-time.

Safe Travel Tips

1. Plan Ahead

When traveling, whether locally or internationally, planning is essential. Research your destination, accommodations, and transportation options in advance. Knowing what to expect can help you avoid potentially risky situations.

2. Secure Your Belongings

Keep your belongings secure at all times, especially in crowded places like airports or train stations. Use anti-theft bags or accessories if necessary. Be cautious of pickpockets and keep essential items like passports and wallets in a concealed, secure location.

3. Stay in Well-Lit Areas

When walking or using public transportation at night, stick to well-lit areas and avoid shortcuts through dark alleys or deserted streets. If possible, travel with a group or use reputable ride-sharing services.

Choose accommodations with good reviews and a solid reputation for safety. Lock your doors and windows when inside your room, and use the door's peephole before opening it to strangers.

Seek advice from locals or hotel staff about safe areas and potential hazards in the area you're visiting. They can provide valuable insights that guide your choices and help you stay safe.

Conclusion

Personal safety is a matter of paramount importance for women, and it's crucial to be proactive and well-prepared. Self-defense techniques and training empower women with the skills and confidence needed to protect themselves in various situations. Developing situational awareness helps identify potential threats and make informed decisions. When traveling, planning ahead, securing belongings, and staying in well-lit areas are essential practices.

It's important to remember that personal safety is not about living in fear but rather about being prepared and vigilant. By taking these proactive steps, women can navigate the world with confidence, knowing they have the knowledge and tools to prioritize their safety. In a society where everyone deserves to live free from fear and harm, personal safety is a fundamental right that women should actively pursue and protect.

Introduction

Safety is a fundamental human need, and ensuring it begins at home and extends to our immediate surroundings. In a world where women often face unique safety challenges, it is essential to take proactive measures to protect oneself and create a secure environment. This article explores the crucial aspects of home and neighborhood safety, providing practical insights and strategies for women to safeguard themselves and their loved ones.

Securing Your Home

1. Locking Systems

The first line of defense for your home is a robust locking system. Invest in high-quality deadbolts and door locks for all entry points. Consider installing a peephole to identify visitors before opening the door. Reinforce sliding doors with bars, and don't forget to secure windows with sturdy locks or shatter-resistant films.

2. Lighting

Well-lit exteriors deter potential intruders. Install motion-activated lights around your property, especially near entrances, pathways, and dark corners. Adequate lighting not only helps prevent break-ins but also ensures your safety when arriving home after dark.

3. Alarm Systems

Modern security systems are highly effective in deterring intruders and notifying you or security professionals of a breach. Choose a system that includes door/window sensors, motion detectors, and, if possible, surveillance cameras. Some systems offer smartphone integration, enabling you to monitor your home remotely.

4. Secure Valuables

Keep valuable items like jewelry, important documents, and electronics in a secure safe or hidden location. This reduces the incentive for burglars and minimizes potential losses in case of a break-in.

5. Home Automation

Smart home technology allows you to control lighting, locks, and alarms remotely. This can be a powerful tool for enhancing security, as you can simulate your presence even when you're away.

Neighborhood Watch Programs

1. Joining or Starting a Neighborhood Watch

Community involvement is key to improving neighborhood safety. Consider joining or initiating a neighborhood watch program. These groups encourage residents to look out for one another, report suspicious activity, and collaborate with local law enforcement to address safety concerns.

2. Building Relationships

Get to know your neighbors and foster a sense of community. Establishing strong relationships with those living nearby can create a supportive network that promotes safety. Neighbors who look out for each other are more likely to notice unusual activity and offer assistance when needed.

3. Communication

Effective communication within the neighborhood is crucial. Establish a reliable method of communication, such as a neighborhood social media group or email list, to quickly share safety tips, updates on local incidents, and other relevant information.

4. Regular Patrols

Organize or participate in regular neighborhood patrols. This proactive approach can help deter criminal activity and make residents feel safer in their own community.

Dealing with Domestic Violence

1. Awareness and Education

Domestic violence is a pervasive issue that affects countless women worldwide. Educate yourself and your loved ones about the signs of domestic abuse, the resources available for victims, and how to offer support. Recognizing the problem is the first step in addressing it.

2. Emergency Escape Plan

If you are in an abusive relationship, develop a comprehensive safety plan that includes a secure escape route, a list of essential documents and belongings to take with you, and a designated safe haven. Share this plan with a trusted friend or family member who can assist you when the need arises.

3. Seek Help

Reach out to organizations and support groups specializing in domestic violence. Many offer confidential hotlines, shelters, counseling services, and legal assistance. Don't hesitate to seek professional help if you are in an abusive situation.

4. Legal Protection

Familiarize yourself with local laws and resources that protect victims of domestic violence. Obtaining restraining orders or protective orders can provide a legal barrier between you and your abuser.

5. Self-Defense Training

Consider enrolling in self-defense classes to build confidence and physical skills to protect yourself in emergency situations. While self-defense should be a last resort, it can be a valuable tool in ensuring your safety.

Conclusion

Safety is a shared responsibility that begins at home and extends to the community. Women's safety is a critical concern, and taking proactive steps to secure your home, engage with your neighborhood, and address domestic violence can make a significant difference in your well-being.

By securing your home with advanced locking systems, adequate lighting, and alarm systems, you create a strong deterrent against potential intruders. Additionally, smart home technology can offer convenience and enhanced security. Joining or starting a neighborhood watch program fosters a sense of community and helps deter crime while building relationships with neighbors.

Dealing with domestic violence is a complex issue that requires awareness, education, and support. It's essential to recognize the signs of abuse, create a safety plan, seek help from support organizations, and be aware of legal protections available to victims. Self-defense training can also provide valuable tools for personal safety.

In conclusion, taking steps to ensure home and neighborhood safety empowers women to lead more secure and confident lives. Remember that your safety is a priority, and by being proactive, informed, and connected with your community, you can create a safer and more secure environment for yourself and those around you.

Introduction

In an increasingly interconnected world, the internet has become an integral part of our lives, offering numerous opportunities and benefits. However, along with the advantages, it has also brought forth new challenges, particularly in the realm of online safety. For women, navigating the digital landscape can be a complex and sometimes hazardous journey. This article explores the various facets of online safety for women, shedding light on issues such as cyberbullying, online harassment, privacy, and security.

Cyberbullying: A Digital Menace

Cyberbullying, a malicious form of online harassment, poses a significant threat to women's safety. It involves the use of digital platforms to target individuals with harmful intent. The anonymity provided by the internet often emboldens perpetrators, making it easier for them to engage in harmful behavior. Women are particularly vulnerable to cyberbullying, and the consequences can be emotionally devastating.

1. Forms of Cyberbullying

Cyberbullying takes various forms, including:

Harassment: Repeated, unwanted messages, comments, or threats can cause severe distress.

Doxxing: The malicious act of revealing personal information, such as addresses and phone numbers, puts women at physical risk.

Impersonation: Impersonating someone online can damage reputations and relationships.

Cyberstalking: Relentless online pursuit can lead to real-life safety concerns.

2. Impact on Mental Health

The emotional toll of cyberbullying cannot be overstated. Women subjected to online harassment often experience anxiety, depression, and reduced self-esteem. The fear of encountering their aggressors online can lead to a sense of isolation and powerlessness.

3. Preventive Measures

To combat cyberbullying, women can take several preventive measures:

Adjust Privacy Settings: Review and tighten your privacy settings on social media platforms to limit the exposure of personal information.

Block and Report: Utilize the blocking and reporting features on social media platforms to curb harassment.

Cybersecurity Awareness: Stay informed about online threats and educate yourself about cybersecurity best practices.

Online Harassment: The Dark Side of Social Media

Online harassment encompasses a wide range of hostile behaviors directed towards individuals online. Women are disproportionately affected by this issue, enduring a barrage of sexist comments, threats, and unsolicited advances. Addressing online harassment is crucial for women's safety and well-being.

1. The Gendered Nature of Online Harassment

Online harassment disproportionately targets women and often manifests as gender-based violence. Sexist comments, body-shaming, and misogynistic abuse create a hostile digital environment that can have real-world consequences.

Body shaming is the act of criticizing, mocking, or making negative comments about a person's physical appearance, often in a hurtful or judgmental way, which can lead to feelings of self-consciousness, low self-esteem, and body image issues for the targeted individual. *Misogynistic abuse* refers to the verbal, psychological, or physical mistreatment and discrimination directed at women or individuals perceived as women, rooted in deep-seated prejudices and hatred against women, often perpetuating gender-based stereotypes and inequality.

2. Impact on Women's Lives

Online harassment can disrupt a woman's life in numerous ways:

Career: Negative online attention can harm professional opportunities and reputations.

Mental Health: Constant exposure to harassment can lead to anxiety, depression, and other mental health issues.

Relationships: Women may hesitate to engage in online communities or dating apps due to fear of harassment.

3. Coping Strategies

Dealing with online harassment requires resilience and strategic responses:

Document: Keep records of all harassing messages, comments, or interactions.

Report: Report harassers to the platform administrators or, in extreme cases, to law enforcement.

Seek Support: Share your experiences with friends, family, or support groups for emotional assistance.

Privacy and Security Online

Privacy and security concerns are central to online safety for women. The digital landscape is rife with opportunities for personal information to be exploited. Women must be proactive in safeguarding their digital presence to avoid falling victim to various forms of cyberattacks.

1. The Value of Privacy

Preserving privacy is crucial for online safety. Here are some key aspects to consider:

Data Protection: Be cautious about sharing personal information, such as your address or phone number, online.

Password Security: Use strong, unique passwords for different accounts and enable two-factor authentication when available.

Social Media: Review your social media profiles and limit the sharing of personal details.

2. Online Security Measures

To enhance online security, women can implement the following measures:

Antivirus Software: Install reputable antivirus software to protect against malware and phishing attacks.

Regular Updates: Keep your operating system, apps, and antivirus software up to date to patch vulnerabilities.

Privacy Tools: Use virtual private networks (VPNs) to encrypt your internet connection and protect your browsing data.

Conclusion

Online safety is an essential concern for women in today's digital world. Cyberbullying and online harassment threaten the emotional well-being of women, while privacy and security issues can have far-reaching consequences. It is imperative for women to be vigilant and proactive in protecting themselves online.

As society continues to grapple with these challenges, raising awareness and promoting digital literacy are key components of improving online safety for women. By adopting preventive measures, seeking support, and demanding accountability from online platforms, women can reclaim their digital spaces and ensure that the internet remains a safe and empowering environment for all. In a world where the virtual and physical realms are increasingly intertwined, online safety is not just an option; it is a necessity for women's well-being and progress.

Introduction

Dating and relationships are an integral part of human life, offering opportunities for love, companionship, and personal growth. However, they can also expose individuals to various risks, including abusive relationships that compromise their safety and well-being. In this comprehensive guide to women's safety, we will explore the complex world of dating and relationships, focusing on recognizing abusive relationships, nurturing healthy relationship dynamics, understanding consent and boundaries, and concluding with essential takeaways for a safer dating experience.

Recognizing Abusive Relationships

1. Types of Abuse

Abusive relationships can take many forms, and it is crucial to recognize them early on. These may include:

Physical abuse: Any form of physical harm or violence.

Emotional abuse: Manipulation, intimidation, or constant criticism.

Verbal abuse: Hurtful words, name-calling, and insults.

Sexual abuse: Non-consensual sexual activities.

Financial abuse: Controlling finances or using money to manipulate.

2. Warning Signs

Identifying the warning signs of an abusive relationship can be challenging, but it's essential to look out for:

> ➤ Frequent criticism and belittlement.
> ➤ Isolation from friends and family.
> ➤ Unreasonable jealousy or possessiveness.
> ➤ Physical aggression or threats.
> ➤ Manipulative behavior and gaslighting.
> ➤ Control over finances and personal choices.

3. Seeking Help

If you or someone you know is in an abusive relationship, don't hesitate to seek help. Reach out to friends, family, or professionals who can provide support and guidance. You deserve a safe and healthy relationship.

Healthy Relationship Dynamics

1. Communication

Effective communication is the cornerstone of a healthy relationship. Open and honest conversations allow partners to express their feelings, needs, and concerns. Active listening is equally crucial; it helps you understand your partner's perspective and fosters empathy.

2. Mutual Respect

Respect forms the foundation of any healthy relationship. It means valuing each other's opinions, boundaries, and autonomy. Respect also involves acknowledging each other's accomplishments and supporting individual goals.

3. Trust

Trust is essential in a relationship. It involves believing in your partner's honesty, integrity, and loyalty. Building trust takes time, but it's crucial for the long-term health of your relationship.

4. Boundaries

Establishing and respecting boundaries is vital to maintaining a healthy relationship. Boundaries are personal limits that define what you're comfortable with, and they can encompass emotional, physical, and sexual boundaries. Discuss boundaries with your partner and ensure that both parties are comfortable and informed.

5. Conflict Resolution

Conflicts are inevitable in any relationship. The key is to address them constructively. Avoiding blame and focusing on finding solutions can help resolve conflicts and strengthen your bond.

Consent and Boundaries

1. Understanding Consent

Consent is a fundamental aspect of any sexual relationship. It means that both partners willingly and enthusiastically agree to engage in any sexual activity. Consent must be explicit, informed, and ongoing. It can be withdrawn at any point, and it should never be assumed.

2. Communication About Boundaries

Discussing boundaries with your partner is crucial to ensure that both parties feel safe and respected. It's essential to communicate your boundaries clearly and to respect your partner's boundaries as well.

3. The Role of Intoxication

Consent cannot be given or obtained if one or both partners are under the influence of alcohol or drugs. It is essential to ensure that both parties are fully aware and capable of giving consent.

4. Consent Education

Promoting consent education is vital in preventing sexual assault. Schools, organizations, and communities should prioritize teaching individuals about the importance of consent, boundaries, and healthy sexual relationships.

5. Consent and Technology

In the digital age, consent extends to online interactions and the sharing of intimate images. Always seek explicit consent before sharing any intimate content and respect your partner's privacy.

Conclusion

Navigating the world of dating and relationships can be both exciting and challenging. While they offer opportunities for connection and personal growth, it's essential to prioritize your safety and well-being. Recognizing the signs of an abusive relationship is the first step towards ensuring your security. Remember that you deserve respect, love, and support in any relationship.

Healthy relationship dynamics involve open communication, mutual respect, trust, and effective conflict resolution. These elements contribute to a fulfilling and nurturing partnership. Additionally, understanding the principles of consent and boundaries is paramount for promoting safe and respectful interactions in any relationship, both in person and online.

In the quest for love and companionship, never compromise your safety or your sense of self-worth. Seek help when needed, surround yourself with supportive individuals, and prioritize your emotional and physical well-being. By following the guidance in this comprehensive guide to women's safety, you can embark on a journey of dating and relationships with confidence, knowing that you are equipped to make informed and empowered choices.

Introduction

Workplace safety is a critical concern for everyone, but it takes on added significance in the context of women's safety. Women constitute a significant portion of the global workforce, contributing their skills, talents, and expertise to various industries. However, they often face unique challenges and vulnerabilities in the workplace. This comprehensive guide to women's safety explores various facets of workplace safety, including sexual harassment prevention, equal pay, workplace discrimination, and reporting workplace issues, with a focus on empowering women to navigate these challenges effectively.

Sexual Harassment Prevention

Sexual harassment is a pervasive issue in many workplaces, and it disproportionately affects women. It creates an unsafe and hostile environment, making it difficult for women to perform their jobs to the best of their abilities. To address this pressing concern, it is essential to promote awareness and establish clear guidelines for sexual harassment prevention.

1. Understanding Sexual Harassment

Sexual harassment can take various forms, including unwelcome advances, comments, or any other conduct of a sexual nature that creates an uncomfortable or hostile environment. It is vital for women to recognize the signs of sexual harassment and understand their rights.

2. Workplace Policies and Training

Employers should implement and communicate strong anti-sexual harassment policies. Regular training programs should educate employees on what constitutes harassment, how to report it, and the consequences for offenders. Women should actively engage in such training to protect themselves and their colleagues.

3. Reporting Mechanisms

Women need to know how and where to report incidents of sexual harassment. Encouraging an open-door policy and offering multiple reporting channels, including anonymous reporting options, can help create a safer work environment.

4. Support Systems

Women should seek out support within their workplace and, if necessary, external organizations. There are various support systems, including HR departments, employee assistance programs, and legal resources, that can provide guidance and assistance.

Equal Pay and Workplace Discrimination

Achieving gender equality in the workplace is not just about addressing overt harassment; it also involves addressing systemic issues like unequal pay and workplace discrimination.

1. Equal Pay

One of the fundamental aspects of women's safety at work is ensuring equal pay for equal work. Despite progress, the gender pay gap persists in many industries. Women must advocate for fair compensation, negotiate their salaries confidently, and hold employers accountable for wage disparities.

2. Workplace Discrimination

Discrimination can manifest in various forms, from subtle biases to overt acts of prejudice. Women must be vigilant about recognizing discrimination and should not hesitate to address it. This includes challenging stereotypes, advocating for promotions and career advancement, and seeking legal recourse if necessary.

3. Mentorship and Networking

Women can benefit from mentorship and networking opportunities to break through gender-related barriers. Establishing relationships with mentors who can offer guidance and support can help women navigate the complex terrain of workplace discrimination.

Reporting Workplace Issues

Reporting workplace issues is an essential step in addressing problems and ensuring a safe and supportive work environment.

1. Confidential Reporting

Many women fear retaliation when reporting workplace issues. Employers should prioritize confidentiality to protect those who come forward. This can be achieved through anonymous reporting systems and clear non-retaliation policies.

2. Documenting Incidents

It's essential for women to document incidents of harassment, discrimination, or any other workplace issues. This can provide evidence and support their case if they decide to take legal action or escalate the matter within the organization.

3. Seeking Legal Advice

In some cases, reporting workplace issues within the organization may not lead to satisfactory resolutions. In such instances, women may need to consult with legal experts to explore their rights and options outside of the workplace.

Conclusion

Workplace safety is a multifaceted issue that affects women in unique ways. Sexual harassment prevention, equal pay, workplace discrimination, and reporting workplace issues are all critical components of ensuring women's safety and empowerment in the modern workplace.

By understanding their rights, advocating for themselves, and actively engaging in initiatives to promote workplace safety, women can help create more inclusive and equitable work environments. It is the collective responsibility of employers, employees, and society as a whole to prioritize women's safety at work and work towards a future where women can thrive without fear or discrimination. Through education, empowerment, and solidarity, we can build workplaces where every woman can reach her full potential.

Introduction

Women's safety is a fundamental human right, and ensuring it requires a multifaceted approach that extends beyond legal and institutional measures. One crucial aspect of women's safety is the establishment and nurturing of robust community and support networks. These networks serve as a safety net, offering emotional, physical, and psychological support to women in times of need. In this comprehensive guide to women's safety, we delve into the significance of community and support networks, exploring the role of support groups and organizations, the process of building a support network, and the importance of engaging with your community.

Support Groups and Organizations

Support groups and organizations play a pivotal role in promoting women's safety by offering a structured platform for individuals to share experiences, seek guidance, and access resources. Here are some key aspects to consider:

Peer Support Groups: Peer support groups, consisting of women who have experienced similar challenges, provide a safe space for sharing stories, emotions, and coping strategies. These groups can address issues ranging from domestic violence to workplace harassment and foster a sense of belonging and understanding.

Nonprofit Organizations: Numerous nonprofit organizations are dedicated to advancing women's safety.

These organizations offer an array of services, such as legal aid, counseling, and crisis intervention. Some well-known examples in the United States include RAINN (Rape, Abuse & Incest National Network) and the National Domestic Violence Hotline.

Local Initiatives: In many communities, grassroots initiatives have emerged to address specific safety concerns. These initiatives might focus on neighborhood safety, self-defense training, or education about women's rights. Joining or supporting such local efforts can have a significant impact.

Building a Support Network

Creating a personal support network is an essential step in enhancing women's safety. Here's how to go about it:

Identify Trusted Individuals: Start by identifying people you trust and feel comfortable confiding in. This could include friends, family members, colleagues, or mentors. Building a support network begins with trust.

Diversify Your Network: Try to diversify your support network to include individuals from different spheres of your life. This ensures that you have a range of perspectives and resources at your disposal.

Establish Open Communication: Open and honest communication is the bedrock of any support network. Let your chosen individuals know that you value their support and are willing to reciprocate when needed.

Set Boundaries: While it's crucial to have a support network, it's equally important to set boundaries. Ensure that your network respects your boundaries and understands when and how to provide assistance.

Seek Professional Help: Don't hesitate to consult professional counselors or therapists if needed. They can provide specialized guidance and support for overcoming trauma, stress, or anxiety.

Engaging with Your Community

Being an active and engaged member of your community is an integral part of women's safety. Here's how you can get involved:

Participate in Neighborhood Watch Programs: Join or initiate neighborhood watch programs to collectively address safety concerns in your area. These programs foster a sense of unity and vigilance, making communities safer.

Advocate for Change: If you come across instances of gender-based violence or discrimination in your community, don't hesitate to speak up and advocate for change. Use your voice to raise awareness and push for policy reforms.

Support Local Women's Shelters: Women's shelters provide refuge to those fleeing abusive situations. Contributing your time, resources, or donations to such organizations can make a significant difference in the lives of survivors.

Promote Education and Awareness: Host workshops, seminars, or awareness campaigns on women's safety topics, such as self-defense techniques, consent education, and recognizing signs of abuse. Education is a powerful tool for prevention.

: Offer mentorship to young women and girls in your community. Empower them with knowledge, skills, and self-confidence to navigate challenges and make informed choices.

Conclusion

Women's safety is a shared responsibility that involves individuals, communities, and society as a whole. Community and support networks are vital components of this effort, providing women with the necessary resources, emotional support, and empowerment to lead safer lives. Whether through peer support groups, nonprofit organizations, or grassroots initiatives, these networks offer solace, guidance, and a sense of belonging.

Building a personal support network is equally essential. Trusting relationships, open communication, and a diverse range of connections can provide the support needed to navigate the complexities of life. Remember that setting boundaries within your network is crucial to maintaining healthy relationships.

Engaging with your community, advocating for change, and supporting local initiatives are actions that can contribute to a safer environment for all women. Active participation in community programs and the promotion of education and awareness are steps toward creating a society where women's safety is prioritized.

In conclusion, women's safety is not just an individual concern but a collective endeavor. By fostering robust community and support networks, we can work together to create a world where women can live, work, and thrive without fear, ensuring that safety is a fundamental right for all.

52

Chapter 10. Mental and Emotional Well-being

Introduction

Women's safety encompasses a wide spectrum of concerns, from physical security to emotional and mental well-being. While much attention has rightly been given to the former, it's equally crucial to address the latter. Mental and emotional well-being plays a significant role in a woman's overall safety and quality of life. This comprehensive guide explores the importance of mental and emotional well-being in the context of women's safety, offering insights into coping with trauma, self-care strategies, and seeking professional help.

Coping with Trauma

Trauma refers to a psychological and emotional response to an event or series of events that are distressing, overwhelming, or harmful, often leading to lasting emotional and psychological effects. Trauma can take many forms, ranging from physical violence to emotional abuse, harassment, or discrimination. Coping with trauma is a crucial aspect of preserving one's mental and emotional well-being.

Recognizing Trauma: The first step in coping with trauma is recognizing it. Many women may downplay their experiences or dismiss them as insignificant. However, acknowledging the impact of traumatic events is essential to begin the healing process.

Seeking Support: It's vital to reach out to a support system that includes friends, family, or support groups. Talking about your experiences and feelings with trusted individuals can help alleviate the emotional burden.

Emotional Expression: Expressing emotions, whether through journaling, art, or therapy, can be cathartic. Bottling up feelings can lead to increased stress and anxiety, hindering mental well-being.

Mindfulness and Meditation: Practices such as mindfulness and meditation can help manage stress and anxiety. They encourage living in the present moment and developing emotional resilience.

Self-Care Strategies

Self-care is an essential component of maintaining mental and emotional well-being. Women must prioritize self-care to build resilience and nurture their mental health.

Establishing Boundaries: Setting clear boundaries in personal and professional relationships is crucial. This helps prevent emotional exhaustion and maintain a sense of control.

Physical Health: A healthy body contributes to a healthy mind. Regular exercise, a balanced diet, and adequate sleep can significantly impact emotional well-being.

Stress Management: Stress is an inevitable part of life, but managing it is key. Techniques like deep breathing, progressive muscle relaxation, and time management can reduce stress levels.

Hobbies and Interests: Pursuing hobbies and interests outside of daily responsibilities can provide a sense of fulfillment and joy.

Positive Self-Talk: Changing negative thought patterns to positive self-talk can improve self-esteem and emotional well-being.

Seeking Professional Help

Sometimes, coping strategies and self-care may not be sufficient to address mental and emotional challenges. Seeking professional help is a sign of strength and a critical step toward ensuring women's mental well-being.

Therapy and Counseling: Therapists and counselors are trained professionals who can provide support and guidance to help women work through their emotional challenges. Individual therapy, group therapy, and counseling services are available to cater to different needs.

Medication: In some cases, mental health conditions may require medication. Psychiatrists can assess the need for medication and prescribe it when necessary.

Support Helplines: Many helplines and crisis centers are available to provide immediate support for individuals facing emotional crises. These services offer a lifeline for those in distress.

Holistic Approaches: Holistic approaches such as acupuncture, yoga, and art therapy can complement traditional forms of therapy and provide alternative avenues for healing.

Conclusion

Women's safety extends beyond physical protection. It encompasses mental and emotional well-being, which are integral components of a woman's overall safety and quality of life. Coping with trauma, self-care strategies, and seeking professional help are essential elements of maintaining mental and emotional health.

By recognizing trauma, seeking support, and expressing emotions, women can take the first steps toward healing. Establishing boundaries, prioritizing physical health, managing stress, and engaging in hobbies contribute to self-care. And when needed, seeking professional help from therapists, counselors, or support helplines is a crucial step toward achieving and maintaining mental and emotional well-being.

Ultimately, a woman's safety is not solely about being protected from external threats; it's also about ensuring that she has the tools and support to navigate the complex landscape of her own mental and emotional world. By addressing mental and emotional well-being, we empower women to lead healthier, more fulfilled lives, and create a safer society for all.

Introduction

Education has always been a powerful tool for personal growth and societal progress. In the context of women's safety and empowerment, education plays a pivotal role in breaking down barriers, fostering self-reliance, and enabling women to take control of their lives. This article explores the multifaceted relationship between education and empowerment, highlighting the ways in which education can transform the lives of women and contribute to their safety and success.

Access to Education and Skill Development

1. Bridging the Gender Gap

Education is often considered the foundation of empowerment, and yet, many women around the world face significant barriers to accessing quality education. Gender disparities in educational opportunities persist in various forms, including limited access to schools, cultural norms that prioritize boys' education, and economic constraints. To address these disparities, governments and NGOs must prioritize policies and initiatives that promote gender equality in education.

2. Early Childhood Education

The journey towards women's empowerment often begins in early childhood. Encouraging girls to pursue education from a young age is crucial. Early childhood education not only lays the groundwork for future learning but also instills confidence and a sense of agency in girls. By providing safe and inclusive spaces for young girls to learn and grow, we set the stage for their future empowerment.

3. Skill Development

Beyond formal education, skill development is a key component of women's empowerment. Equipping women with practical skills, such as vocational training, financial literacy, and digital literacy, can empower them to participate in the workforce and gain economic independence. Skill development programs tailored to women's needs can bridge the gender gap in employment opportunities and financial stability.

Women's Empowerment Initiatives

1. Economic Empowerment

One of the most tangible ways education empowers women is by opening doors to economic opportunities. When women receive an education, they are better equipped to access higher-paying jobs, become entrepreneurs, and contribute to household incomes. Microfinance programs and business development initiatives can further support women in achieving economic independence.

2. Health and Well-being

Education plays a crucial role in improving women's health and well-being. Educated women are more likely to make informed decisions about their health, seek medical care when needed, and access family planning services. Educational initiatives that focus on reproductive health and women's rights can empower women to take control of their bodies and lives.

3. Political Participation

Education empowers women not only in the economic sphere but also in the political arena. Informed and educated women are more likely to engage in political processes, vote, and run for public office. Women's representation in government is essential for addressing gender-based violence and enacting policies that promote women's safety.

Role Models and Success Stories

1. Inspirational Figures

Role models play a significant role in motivating women to pursue education and empowerment. Throughout history, there have been countless women who have broken barriers and shattered stereotypes through their achievements. Figures like Malala Yousafzai, who advocated for girls' education despite adversity, serve as inspirations for women around the world.

2. Local Heroes

It's not just global figures who inspire change; many local heroes are making a difference in their communities. Women who have overcome challenges and achieved success through education can serve as powerful examples for others. Sharing these success stories can motivate and guide young women on their own paths to empowerment.

3. Mentorship Programs

Mentorship programs that connect aspiring women with experienced mentors can be instrumental in fostering empowerment. These programs provide guidance, support, and a sense of belonging, helping women navigate the challenges they may encounter on their educational and career journeys.

Conclusion

Education and empowerment are inseparable partners on the journey to women's safety and success. Access to education and skill development opportunities is the foundation upon which women can build their futures. Initiatives that promote gender equality in education, improve economic prospects, and enhance health and well-being are essential for empowering women.

Furthermore, role models and success stories serve as beacons of hope, demonstrating that obstacles can be overcome and dreams can be realized through education and determination. Mentorship programs provide the necessary support and guidance to help women along their paths to empowerment.

As we continue to strive for a world where women are safe and empowered, we must recognize the pivotal role of education in this endeavor. By investing in the education of women and girls, we are not only breaking down barriers but also fostering a society where women can thrive, lead, and contribute meaningfully to their communities and the world at large. Education is not just a means to an end; it is a powerful force for positive change, paving the way for a brighter, safer, and more equitable future for all women.

Introduction

In a world where women's safety remains a pressing concern, advocacy and policy change play pivotal roles in addressing and combatting the myriad challenges women face daily. This comprehensive guide to women's safety delves into the critical aspects of government and policy advocacy, shedding light on how advocacy efforts can lead to meaningful change for women's rights and safety. Advocacy has the power to not only raise awareness but also influence policymakers, shape legislation, and ultimately create safer environments for women everywhere.

Advocacy for Change

Advocacy, at its core, is the process of speaking up, raising awareness, and fighting for a cause. In the context of women's safety, advocacy is a potent tool for highlighting issues and inspiring change. Here, we explore the multifaceted approaches to advocacy that individuals, organizations, and communities can employ to drive change.

Raising Awareness: Advocacy begins with spreading awareness about the challenges women face concerning their safety. It involves disseminating information, sharing stories, and utilizing various media platforms to educate society about the scope and urgency of the issue. Raising awareness serves as the foundation upon which all other advocacy efforts are built.

Community Engagement: Grassroots advocacy involves engaging with local communities to foster support and build a collective voice for women's safety. Empowering community members to become advocates themselves can have a cascading effect, mobilizing more people to take action.

Online Activism: The digital age has ushered in new avenues for advocacy. Social media, online petitions, and digital campaigns enable advocates to reach a global audience and build momentum for their cause. Hashtags, viral videos, and online platforms amplify the voices of women, making it difficult for policymakers to ignore their demands.

Lobbying for Women's Rights

Lobbying is a vital aspect of advocacy that focuses on influencing policymakers and legislators to enact meaningful change. When it comes to women's safety, lobbying efforts target both government officials and lawmakers to ensure that policies and laws are in place to protect women's rights and safety.

Policy Research and Analysis: Effective lobbying begins with a deep understanding of existing policies and their impact on women's safety. Advocates and organizations conduct research, gather data, and analyze legislation to identify gaps and areas in need of improvement.

Coalitions and Alliances: Forming coalitions and alliances with like-minded organizations and individuals enhances lobbying efforts. Strength in numbers can bring greater attention to the cause and increase the chances of policymakers taking action.

Direct Engagement: Advocates can engage directly with policymakers through meetings, hearings, and consultations. Sharing personal stories and data-backed evidence can be persuasive in driving home the importance of women's safety measures.

Advocacy Campaigns: Lobbying often involves sustained advocacy campaigns targeting specific legislation or policy changes. These campaigns utilize various tactics, such as public demonstrations, letter-writing campaigns, and grassroots mobilization, to put pressure on decision-makers.

Engaging with Policymakers

To effect real change, advocates must engage with policymakers in a constructive and strategic manner. Building relationships with government officials and lawmakers can be a challenging but essential aspect of the advocacy process.

Building Bridges: Advocates should seek opportunities to build relationships with policymakers who are sympathetic to the cause of women's safety. These connections can provide valuable insights and open doors for advocacy efforts.

Educating Policymakers: Many policymakers may not be fully aware of the extent of the issues surrounding women's safety. Advocates can play a crucial role in educating them, presenting evidence, and providing expert guidance on potential solutions.

Public Pressure: Policymakers are often responsive to public pressure and the will of their constituents. Advocacy campaigns that mobilize the public can be highly effective in pressuring policymakers to take action.

Policy Proposals: Advocates can contribute to the policymaking process by developing and proposing specific policies and legislative changes aimed at improving women's safety. These proposals should be well-researched and evidence-based.

Conclusion

Government and policy advocacy are integral components of the ongoing effort to enhance women's safety. As we have explored in this comprehensive guide, advocacy serves as the catalyst for change, raising awareness, inspiring action, and shaping policies that protect women's rights and well-being.

While progress has been made in many parts of the world, there is still much work to be done. Women continue to face a wide range of safety challenges, from gender-based violence to workplace discrimination. Effective advocacy and lobbying efforts are essential to address these issues comprehensively.

Advocacy is not a one-size-fits-all approach. It requires a multifaceted strategy that includes raising awareness, community engagement, online activism, lobbying, and direct engagement with policymakers. Building bridges with policymakers and educating them about the pressing need for change can lead to more effective policy decisions and legislative reforms.

In conclusion, government and policy advocacy are powerful tools in the fight for women's safety. The collective efforts of advocates, organizations, and communities can drive meaningful change, ensuring that women are not only safe but also empowered to live their lives to the fullest. By continuing to work tirelessly and strategically, we can create a world where women's safety is a fundamental human right, and no woman lives in fear or insecurity.

Introduction

In an increasingly interconnected world, the issue of women's safety transcends borders and cultures, making it a matter of global concern. Women's safety is not just a local or national issue; it's a universal challenge that impacts women across the globe. This article delves into the multifaceted dimensions of women's safety on a global scale, exploring the issues women face worldwide, international efforts and organizations working to address these issues, and the critical cross-cultural considerations that shape the discourse.

Women's Safety Issues Worldwide

Gender-Based Violence: Gender-based violence is a pervasive global issue that affects women in every corner of the world. It includes physical, sexual, psychological, and economic abuse. According to the World Health Organization (WHO), approximately one in three women worldwide has experienced physical or sexual intimate partner violence or non-partner sexual violence in their lifetime.

Human Trafficking: Women and girls are disproportionately affected by human trafficking, often forced into prostitution, forced labor, or other forms of exploitation. This modern-day slavery is a grave violation of women's safety and dignity, and it transcends international borders.

Child Marriage and Female Genital Mutilation: Child marriage and female genital mutilation are practices that rob girls of their agency and safety. They persist in many parts of the world, affecting millions of girls and women.

Access to Education: In some regions, girls' access to education is limited or denied altogether. Lack of education can perpetuate cycles of poverty and restrict opportunities for personal and economic growth, impacting women's safety.

Economic Empowerment: Economic inequality between genders is a global issue. Women often face wage gaps, limited access to financial resources, and economic dependence, which can hinder their ability to escape abusive situations.

International Efforts and Organizations

United Nations (UN) Initiatives: The United Nations has been at the forefront of global efforts to address women's safety issues. The UN has adopted various resolutions and frameworks, including the Convention on the Elimination of All Forms of Discrimination Against Women (CEDAW) and the Sustainable Development Goals (SDGs), which include gender equality and women's empowerment as key targets.

UN Women: UN Women is a specialized UN agency dedicated to gender equality and the empowerment of women. It works globally to promote gender-responsive policies, eliminate violence against women, and advance women's economic empowerment.

Non-Governmental Organizations (NGOs): Numerous NGOs, such as Amnesty International, Human Rights Watch, and Plan International, operate globally to advocate for women's rights and safety. They provide support to survivors, conduct research, and raise awareness about women's safety issues.

International Agreements and Treaties: International agreements like the Istanbul Convention on preventing and combating violence against women and domestic violence, and the Palermo Protocol on human trafficking, set global standards for combating gender-based violence and human trafficking.

Global Campaigns: Initiatives like the #MeToo movement and HeForShe have transcended national boundaries, sparking conversations and activism on women's safety and gender equality on a global scale.

Cross-Cultural Considerations

Diverse Cultural Norms: Cultural norms and traditions vary significantly across the globe. What may be considered acceptable behavior in one culture could be seen as a violation of women's safety in another. Understanding and respecting these differences is crucial when addressing women's safety issues.

Legal Frameworks: The legal framework surrounding women's rights and safety differs from country to country. Some nations have comprehensive laws in place to protect women, while others lack such protections. The enforcement of existing laws can also vary widely.

Religious Influence: In some societies, religious beliefs and practices can either support or hinder women's safety. Religious leaders and institutions can play a significant role in shaping societal attitudes and behaviors towards women.

Economic Disparities: Economic disparities can impact women's safety differently in various cultures. In some cultures, women's financial independence is encouraged, while in others, women are expected to rely on male family members for support.

Language and Communication: Effective communication is crucial for addressing women's safety issues. Language barriers can hinder women from seeking help or reporting abuse. It is essential to provide information and support in multiple languages to ensure accessibility.

Conclusion

The issue of women's safety is a global concern that transcends borders, cultures, and socioeconomic backgrounds. Gender-based violence, human trafficking, child marriage, and other safety-related issues affect women in every corner of the world. International efforts, spearheaded by organizations like the United Nations and NGOs, have made significant strides in addressing these challenges. However, the path to achieving women's safety on a global scale is complex, with cross-cultural considerations playing a pivotal role.

Understanding diverse cultural norms, legal frameworks, religious influences, economic disparities, and language barriers is essential for crafting effective strategies to ensure women's safety worldwide. It requires a nuanced approach that respects local contexts while upholding universal human rights principles. Only through collaborative efforts, a commitment to gender equality, and a determination to dismantle the structures perpetuating gender-based violence can we hope to create a safer world for all women. Ultimately, women's safety is not just a women's issue - it is a global imperative that requires the collective action of individuals, communities, and nations to bring about lasting change.

Introduction

Violence against women is a global epidemic that transcends cultural, economic, and geographic boundaries. It is a grave violation of human rights, perpetuating a cycle of fear, pain, and suffering for countless women around the world. Addressing this issue requires a multifaceted approach that includes early intervention programs, preventive measures, and the promotion of gender equality. In this comprehensive guide, we will delve into these crucial aspects of preventing violence against women.

Early Intervention Programs

1. Awareness and Education

One of the fundamental strategies in preventing violence against women is early intervention through awareness and education. By educating communities, schools, and families about the signs and consequences of violence, we can empower individuals to recognize and report abusive behaviors.

Education programs should target both women and men, emphasizing the importance of healthy relationships, consent, and respect. Schools play a pivotal role in this effort by incorporating comprehensive sex education into their curricula, promoting understanding, empathy, and open communication.

Establishing crisis helplines and support services is essential for women facing immediate danger or seeking help to escape abusive situations. These services provide a lifeline for survivors, offering guidance, safety planning, and access to resources such as shelters, legal aid, and counseling.

Public awareness campaigns can promote these services, ensuring that survivors know where to turn for help and that they will be met with compassion and assistance. Governments and NGOs should work together to fund and expand these vital resources.

Preventive Measures

1. Legal Reforms

Strong legal frameworks are a cornerstone of preventing violence against women. Laws that criminalize various forms of violence, including domestic abuse, sexual harassment, and human trafficking, create a deterrent effect. Additionally, they provide survivors with legal recourse and a means of seeking justice.

To enhance preventive measures, governments should continually review and update legislation to address emerging challenges. This may include harsher penalties for perpetrators, the removal of legal loopholes, and protective orders that keep abusers away from their victims.

2. Community Policing

Community policing strategies can help build trust between law enforcement and communities, making it easier for survivors to report incidents of violence. By fostering cooperation, officers can better respond to cases and ensure the safety of those affected.

Training for law enforcement should include sensitivity to gender-based violence issues, enabling officers to handle cases with empathy and understanding. Building bridges between the police and marginalized communities is critical for addressing the root causes of violence.

3. Economic Empowerment

Economic vulnerability often exacerbates violence against women. Economic empowerment initiatives, such as job training programs and microfinance opportunities, can empower women to become financially independent, reducing their reliance on abusive partners.

Governments and NGOs can support these initiatives by providing funding, resources, and mentorship programs for women looking to start their own businesses or secure stable employment. Empowered women are less likely to remain in abusive relationships due to financial dependence.

Promoting Gender Equality

1. Challenging Stereotypes

Promoting gender equality requires challenging harmful stereotypes and traditional gender roles that perpetuate violence. Society often imposes expectations on women and men, limiting their choices and opportunities. By encouraging diverse and inclusive representations of gender, we can challenge these norms and reduce the incidence of violence.

Media, schools, and community organizations can play a significant role in promoting gender equality by depicting strong, non-stereotypical role models and educating the public about the harmful effects of gender bias.

2. Empowering Women's Voices

Empowering women's voices is essential in the fight against violence. Women must have a platform to share their experiences, advocate for their rights, and influence policies that affect their lives. Through initiatives like women's leadership programs and women's shelters, we can empower women to become agents of change.

By amplifying the voices of survivors and advocates, we can raise awareness about the prevalence of violence and inspire communities to take action. Empowered women become advocates for change, contributing to the overall reduction of violence.

Conclusion

Preventing violence against women is a multifaceted challenge that requires collective effort and commitment from governments, communities, and individuals. Early intervention programs, preventive measures, and the promotion of gender equality are all integral components of a comprehensive strategy to combat this issue.

It is imperative that society recognizes the urgency of this problem and takes decisive action to address it. By raising awareness, educating the public, implementing legal reforms, and promoting gender equality, we can create a safer and more equitable world for women. Violence against women should not be tolerated in any form, and our collective efforts can help break the cycle of abuse, ensuring a brighter, safer future for all women.

Chapter 15. Conclusion and Call to Action

As we reach the final chapter of "A Comprehensive Guide to Women's Safety", it is imperative to reflect on the journey we have embarked upon, one that has explored the multifaceted dimensions of women's safety and security. This book has taken us through various chapters, each addressing critical aspects of this pressing issue. From understanding the threats women face to legal frameworks, personal safety, online safety, relationships, workplace dynamics, and more, we have covered a wide spectrum of knowledge. Now, in this concluding chapter, we shall summarize the key points, encourage action, and ignite hope for a safer and more equitable future.

Summarizing Key Points

1. Understanding the Complexity of Women's Safety

Women's safety is a complex issue, encompassing physical, emotional, and online threats. It is not confined to one's personal space but extends to the workplace, community, and even the global context. By acknowledging the diversity of these challenges, we take the first step towards effective solutions.

2. Legal Frameworks and Personal Empowerment

The legal framework plays a crucial role in safeguarding women's rights. Knowledge of existing laws and avenues for legal recourse empowers women to seek justice and protection. However, personal empowerment through self-defense, situational awareness, and building support networks is equally vital in navigating the complex landscape of safety.

3. Safety in Relationships and the Workplace

Healthy relationships are built on mutual respect, consent, and boundaries. Recognizing abusive dynamics and reporting them is essential for women's safety in intimate relationships. In the workplace, addressing issues like sexual harassment and discrimination is crucial for creating safe and inclusive environments.

4. Community Support and Mental Well-being

Support groups and community engagement provide a network of assistance and solidarity. Additionally, addressing mental and emotional well-being is vital for healing and resilience. Seeking professional help when needed is a sign of strength, not weakness.

5. Education, Empowerment, and Advocacy

Education is the foundation of empowerment. Access to education and skill development programs enables women to break barriers and achieve their potential. Moreover, advocacy and engagement with policymakers are indispensable in driving systemic change.

6. Preventing Violence and Promoting Equality

Prevention is key to reducing violence against women. Early intervention programs and initiatives aimed at promoting gender equality are essential components of a safer future.

Encouraging Readers to Take Action

Empowerment and change begin with each one of us. The knowledge and insights gained from this book serve as a catalyst for action. Here are some steps you can take to contribute to women's safety:

1. Raise Awareness

Start conversations about women's safety in your community, workplace, and online. By increasing awareness, we can create a more supportive environment for those who need it.

2. Educate Yourself and Others

Continue learning about women's safety issues, not just for your benefit but also to educate others. Knowledge is a powerful tool for change.

3. Support Women in Need

Be there for women who may be experiencing threats or violence. Offer your support, and encourage them to seek help if necessary. You could be a lifeline.

4. Advocate for Change

Engage with local, national, and international organizations advocating for women's rights and safety. Join movements that align with your values and become a voice for change.

5. Promote Healthy Relationships

In your personal life, promote healthy relationships built on respect, consent, and open communication. Be a role model for those around you.

6. Work Towards Gender Equality

Support initiatives aimed at achieving gender equality, whether it's through workplace diversity programs, educational scholarships, or community projects.

7. Invest in Your Mental and Emotional Well-being

Remember that taking care of yourself is essential to being able to help others. Seek professional help if needed, and prioritize your mental and emotional well-being.

8. Encourage Policy Change

Engage with policymakers and advocate for changes in laws and policies that can better protect women's rights and safety.

Inspiring Hope and Change

It is natural to feel overwhelmed by the magnitude of the challenges women face when it comes to safety and security. However, we must remember that change is possible, and history has shown us that progress is achievable.

1. Individual Acts of Courage

Countless individuals have shown incredible courage in the face of adversity. Their stories inspire hope and remind us that even small acts of bravery can spark significant change.

2. Collective Action

Throughout history, social movements have transformed societies. By joining forces with others who share our commitment to women's safety, we can effect change on a broader scale.

3. The Power of Education

Education has been a driving force behind societal progress. When we invest in the education and empowerment of women, we invest in a brighter, safer future for all.

4. Policy Reforms

Legal reforms have played a pivotal role in advancing women's rights. By advocating for changes in policies and laws, we can create a more just and equal world.

5. Global Solidarity

Women's safety is a global issue. By fostering international cooperation and solidarity, we can address systemic challenges that transcend borders.

Conclusion

In closing, "A Comprehensive Guide to Women's Safety" has provided us with a comprehensive understanding of the challenges women face and the tools and knowledge needed to address them. Women's safety is not just a women's issue; it's a human issue that requires collective action.

As you embark on your journey to contribute to women's safety, remember that every effort, no matter how small, makes a difference. By raising awareness, educating yourself and others, supporting women in need, advocating for change, and promoting healthy relationships, you can be a part of the solution.

Let us work together to create a world where every woman can live free from fear, where her rights and safety are protected, and where gender equality is not just a goal but a reality.

The path ahead may be challenging, but it is also filled with hope and the promise of a brighter future. Together, we can make that future a reality. The time for action is now.

Thank you for joining us on this journey towards a safer, more inclusive world for all women. Your commitment and dedication are the driving forces behind the change we seek. Let us move forward with determination, compassion, and hope, knowing that together, we can empower women's safety and security, one step at a time.

In "A Comprehensive Guide to Women's Safety", readers embark on a vital journey through the multifaceted realm of women's safety and security. This enlightening book delves into the intricacies of the subject, offering a well-rounded exploration of topics that range from the historical context of women's safety to the global perspective on the issue.

With a keen focus on empowerment and action, the book's chapters provide valuable insights into understanding threats, navigating the legal landscape, ensuring personal and online safety, fostering healthy relationships, and engaging in advocacy for change. As an indispensable resource, this guide not only educates but also motivates, urging readers to become agents of change in their communities and championing the cause of women's safety.

ABOUT THE AUTHOR

Mr. C. P. Kumar is a retired Scientist 'G' from National Institute of Hydrology, Roorkee, Uttarakhand, India. He is also a Reiki Healer and Chakra Balancing practitioner (with pendulum dowsing) and offers Emotional Freedom Technique (EFT) to help individuals with emotional issues. Mr. Kumar has authored many books on technical, spiritual, and social topics.

For further details, you may visit his webpage
https://www.angelfire.com/nh/cpkumar/virgo.html